Jesus Loves

Stories about Jesus for Children

Written by Ron and Lyn Klug
Illustrated by Paul Konsterlie

Augsburg Publishing House, Minneapolis

Dear Parents:

In a familiar, old hymn we sing, "I love to tell the story . . . the old, old story of Jesus and his love." In the life of Jesus the love of God broke into human history in a new way as Jesus "went about doing good."

In this book we have selected some of the many events that show Jesus teaching, healing the sick, feeding the hungry, and comforting those who are sad or frightened. As you read the book with your child, you might ask, "What are some ways Jesus showed love to people?" Then ask, "How can we show love to people today?"

This book is the second of three books that recount the life of Jesus for young children. Jesus Comes *tells the story of Jesus' birth and the ways in which he comes to us today.* Jesus Lives! *focuses on the suffering, death, and resurrection of Jesus, and how he lives with us now.*

JESUS LOVES
Stories about Jesus for Children

LCCC 86-81807 ISBN 0-8066-2235-0

Manufactured in the U.S.A. APH 10-3526

2 3 4 5 6 7 8 9 0 1 2 3 4 5 6 7 8 9

When Jesus was grown-up, he came to the Jordan River to be baptized.

God said, "You are my Son. I am pleased with you."

Then Jesus began to show how much he loved people by helping them in many ways.

One day Jesus was walking along a lake and saw some fishermen.

He said, "Come, follow me, and be my helpers."

The fishermen left their boats and their nets and followed Jesus. Jesus chose 12 men, who were called his disciples. They went with Jesus and helped him.

Jesus was a good storyteller. Both children and grown-ups loved to hear his stories.

Once, so many people came to hear Jesus that he had to teach them from a boat near shore.

Once, when Jesus was out in the fields, he looked around at the flowers blooming and at the birds flying. "Look how God takes care of the flowers and the birds," he said to the people who were with him. "God cares for you, too."

Jesus taught his followers to pray. "God loves you," he told them. "God wants you to talk with him about everything that is important to you."

Jesus went to a place far out in the country to be alone with his disciples. But more than 5000 people followed Jesus. They wanted to hear him tell about God's love.

When it began to get dark, the disciples said to Jesus, "The people are hungry. A boy here has offered to share his food. He has five pieces of bread and two fish, but that's not enough for all these people!" Jesus took the boy's food and thanked God for it. The disciples began to hand it out. And there was enough for everyone!

Once, Jesus' disciples were out fishing. They worked all night, but they didn't catch any fish.

Jesus said, "Go out into the deep water and let down your nets." The disciples did as Jesus said, and suddenly their nets were bursting with fish.

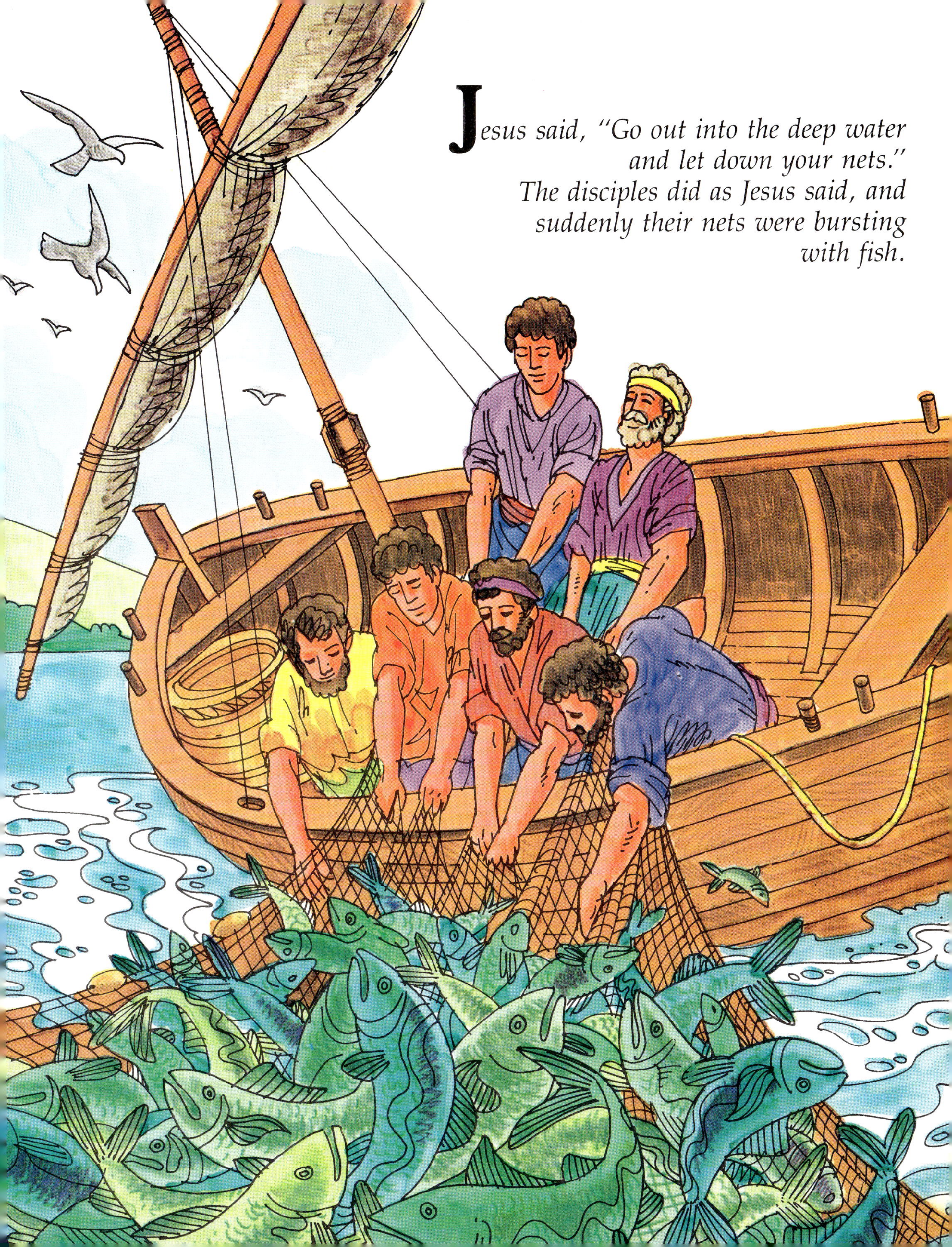

There were so many fish that they had to call for their partners in another boat to help.

Another time Jesus found a blind man
begging by the roadside.
The man called out, "Jesus,
please help me!"

What do you want me to do for you?" Jesus asked.

"Oh, I wish I could see!" the man replied.

"Because you believe in me, you are healed," Jesus said.

Immediately the man could see, and he followed Jesus.

One day some mothers
brought their children
to see Jesus.
They wanted Jesus to pray
for the children
and bless them.
But Jesus' disciples said
to the women,
"Jesus is too busy now.
Please don't bother him."

When Jesus heard them, he said, "Don't send the children away. I love them, and I want them to be near me."

He took the children in his lap and blessed them.

There was a man named Zacchaeus, who had no friends. When he heard that Jesus was coming, he went to meet him.

But he couldn't see because there were so many people and because Zacchaeus was too small.

Then Zacchaeus had an idea! He climbed high up in a tree.

When Jesus came near the tree, he looked up and said, "Zacchaeus, come on down. I want to be your friend."

Jesus went to stay at Zacchaeus' home. Zacchaeus was very happy!

A father came to see Jesus and said, "My little girl is very sick, and I'm afraid she will die. Please come and make her well."

Together Jesus and the man hurried to the house where the little girl was.

But while they were on the way,
some people came running up and said,
"Your daughter has already died."
"Don't be afraid," Jesus said.
"Only trust me."

When they came to the man's house, Jesus took the mother and father into the room where the little girl was lying. "Little girl!" he said. "Get up!" The girl got up and started walking around. "Give her something to eat," Jesus said.

Sometimes Jesus showed his love by helping people when they were afraid. Once, when Jesus was in a boat with his disciples, he fell asleep. A big storm came up, and the disciples were afraid the boat would sink.

The disciples woke Jesus.
"Help us!" they cried. "We're going to drown."
"Don't be afraid," Jesus said.
And he made the wind and waves be still.

These are only some of the ways
Jesus showed his love for people.
He even loved us so much
that he died on the cross for us.
God raised Jesus from the dead
and gave him new life.

Before Jesus left the earth, he told his disciples that they could share his love by teaching and healing and helping others.

Today Jesus still loves us and helps us.

Jesus teaches us through his Word. He has helpers like parents and teachers and pastors.

When we're sick,
Jesus heals us.
Doctors and nurses are Jesus' helpers.

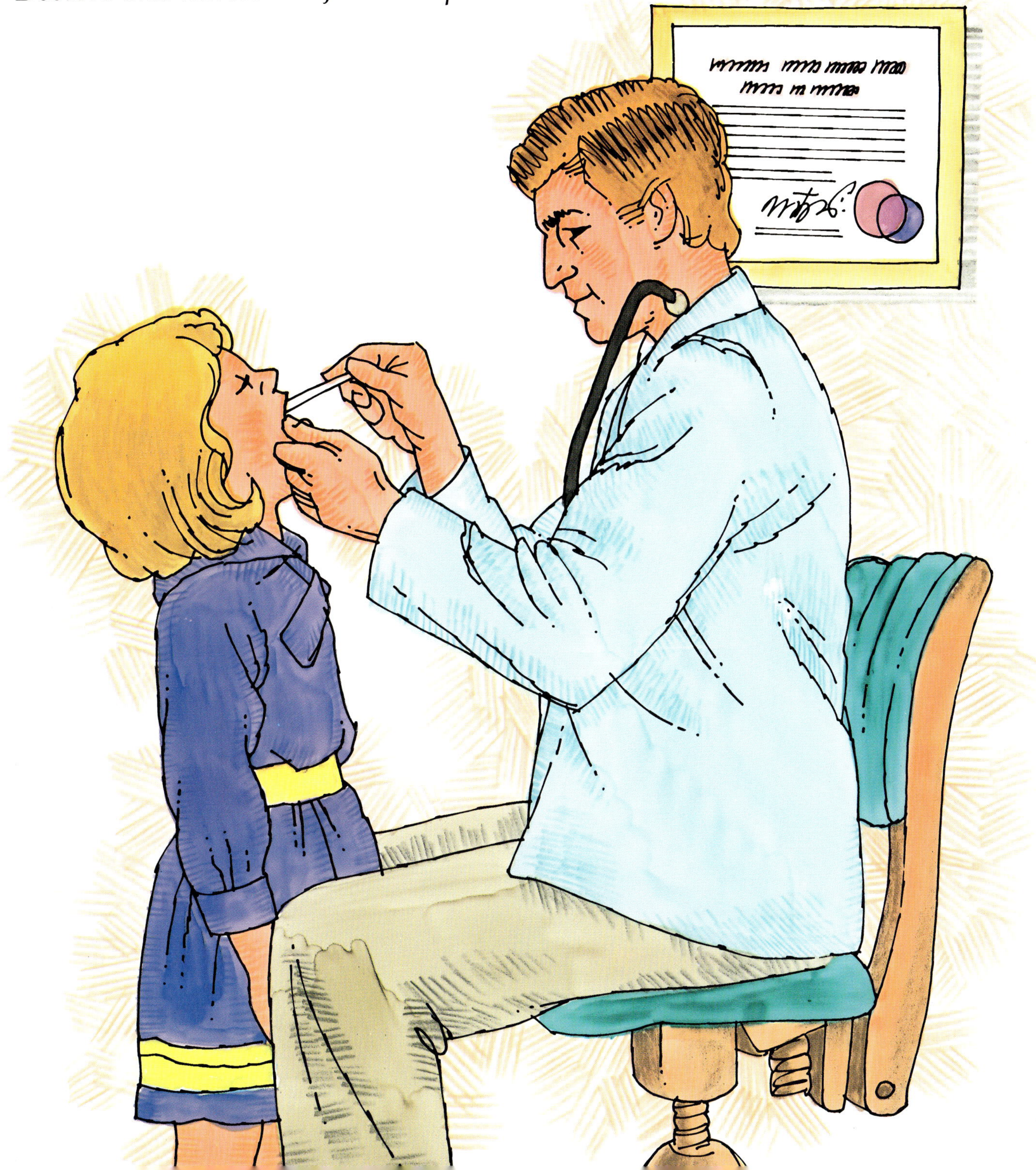

Jesus still gives food
to the hungry.
Farmers and store owners
and truck drivers and many others
help to get food to hungry people.

Jesus loves all people
and wants to be their friend.
When we're afraid,
Jesus sends someone to comfort us.

You are Jesus' helper too.
You share God's love whenever
you help someone
and make them happy.